HOLLYWOOD CHRISTMAS

EDITED BY J. C. SUARÈS

TEXT BY J. SPENCER BECK

THOMASSON · GRANT

Published by Thomasson-Grant, Inc.

Copyright © 1994 J. C. Suarès.
Captions copyright © 1994 J. Spencer Beck.

Printed in Hong Kong.

ISBN 1-56566-069-2

00 99 98 97 96 95 94 5 4 3 2 1

Inquiries should be directed to:
Thomasson-Grant, Inc.
One Morton Drive, Suite 500
Charlottesville, VA 22903-6806
(804) 977-1780

Rita Hayworth, 1945

*At the peak of her popularity as Hollywood's
reigning erotic queen, the soon-to-be ex-Mrs. Orson Welles posed
Tinseltown-style in a leopard-print wrap for a little pre-holiday
Columbia Pictures publicity. Set to star in that company's Technicolor
production of* Tonight and Every Night, *the one-time dancer
born Margarita Cansino would become a love-goddess legend
the following year as the sultry star of* Gilda.

I n "Tinsel"town, where glitter is a year-round way of life, Christmas has always been the biggest (and most profitable) season of the year. The powers that be in "Holly"wood learned early on that movie fans love to mix a little movie-going with their holiday shopping, and films celebrating the season have been moneymakers since the silent era.

Filmed in sun-baked southern California and often substituting plastic flakes for snow, hundreds of Christmastime classics such as *Miracle on 34th Street* and *Holiday Inn* have managed to fuel our holiday fantasies better than any real-life New England Christmas ever could and have made stars of their leading players in the process.

Although many of the studios' lesser efforts feature winter wonderlands that are anything but, white Christmases were created realistically—and at enormous expense—for films such as *Christmas in Connecticut* and *It's a Wonderful Life*. For the latter, actors suffered in record-breaking heat swaddled in sweaters and coats, while crew members scurried to replace tons of real melting snow that had been imported from the Sierra Nevada mountains. The trouble was worth it and helped make the Frank Capra-directed RKO classic the most endearing (and enduring) Christmas movie of all time.

Although there are a number of holiday pictures that revolve around the event itself (at least six versions of Charles Dickens's *A Christmas Carol*; the carbon-copy Bing Crosby vehicles, *Holiday Inn* and *White Christmas*; *A Holiday Affair*; *A Christmas Story*; and *Home Alone*, the biggest-grossing comedy of all time), there are countless films that feature a Christmastime scene or two that will forever make them honorary holiday classics (*Shop Around the Corner, Blossoms in the Dust, The Great Ziegfeld, Bright Eyes, The Story of Alexander Graham Bell*, to name a few). There is even one memorable mid-summer yuletide celebration that tops its traditional counterparts for sheer enthusiasm (*Christmas in July*). In Hollywood, it's never too early to start the season off with a bang.

Of course, not every big-screen Christmas story is a big-box-office smash. There have been at least as many bombs, whose release must have made Santa blush from head to toe. Pat Boone's bare-chested rendition of the title tune in the inappropriately named holiday-season schlocker *April Love* would certainly be more fitting for Valentine's Day, while Debbie Reynolds's turn as a juvenile delinquent who falls in love with a married man in *Susan Slept Here* is hardly family fare for the holidays. And unless you like your Christmas especially campy, *Santa Claus Conquers the Martians* (starring a seven-year-old Pia Zadora in her film debut!) is one low-budget stocking-stuffer better left unwrapped.

These are the exceptions, however. The elves out in Tinseltown have worked hard over the years to create movie magic in a number of sentimental screen classics. Decked out with glittering stars and brimming with more seasonal cheer than Old Saint Nick himself, these films are holiday gifts that will be treasured for all time. Maybe it's the palm trees. Or just the Christmastime profits. But no one dreams of a white Christmas harder than Hollywood.

Danny Kaye and Anne Whitfield

WHITE CHRISTMAS, 1954

*Because Irving Berlin's title tune had already become a holiday
classic twelve years earlier, it was the songwriter's less-than-catchy
"Count Your Blessings Instead of Sheep" that picked up an Oscar
nomination. A rather uninspired remake of* Holiday Inn, *this
Christmas-cheer-filled charmer became a perennial crowd-pleaser,
thanks largely to the talents of its two musical stars,
Bing Crosby and Rosemary Clooney.*

Macaulay Culkin

HOME ALONE, 1990

*Despite its subtle subtext of child abuse and some sadistic
slapstick, this modern Christmas classic about a child accidentally
left alone during the holidays became the biggest-grossing movie of
1990 and the most lucrative film comedy of all time. It also made
its elfin nine-year-old star a mini movie mogul overnight.*

Loretta Young and Don Ameche
THE STORY OF ALEXANDER GRAHAM BELL, 1939
Although he would not win his only Oscar until forty-six years later
for Cocoon, *the law student-turned-actor born Dominic Felix Amici*
became so identified with his role in this Twentieth Century-Fox biopic
about the inventor of the telephone that "I'll call you on the Ameche" became
a popular phrase of the day. As decorous as always, decorating a Christmas
tree in one of the film's more heartwarming scenes, the saintly, apple-cheeked
Young would trim another holiday tree almost half a century later in the
made-for-TV Christmas Eve, *her last screen appearance.*

Geraldine Chaplin

Dr. Zhivago, 1965

*The twenty-year-old Swiss-educated former ballet dancer
and eldest daughter of Charlie Chaplin was perfectly cast as the
elegant if overly refined wife of the title character in this lushly
produced Russian Revolution epic from David Lean. During the
magnificently staged holiday gala at the beginning of the film, she
meets her rival-in-waiting (Julie Christie) for the first time when
the latter crashes the party bearing a decidedly un-Christian
Christmas gift for an erstwhile lover (Rod Steiger).*

**John Payne, Maureen O'Hara,
Natalie Wood, and Edmund Gwenn**
MIRACLE ON 34TH STREET, 1947

*Even sweet-faced little Susan Walker (Wood) finds the idea of Santa
Claus silly at the beginning of this sentimental seasonal favorite from
Twentieth Century-Fox. The picture that did more than any window
display to boost Christmas sales at Macy's department store softened the
hearts of Santa-scoffers around the world with the immortal line:
"Faith is believing in something that common sense tells you not to."*

Donna Reed and James Stewart
IT'S A WONDERFUL LIFE, 1946

*Based on a story that a writer—Philip Van Doren Stern—
had sent to his friends as a Christmas card, this Frank "Capra-corn"
classic about a man saved from a Christmas Eve suicide by a guardian
angel is Hollywood's greatest holiday gift of all time. In no mood
for tree trimming after learning he has just gone bankrupt,
Stewart turns as sour as Scrooge before discovering the true
meaning of Christmas by the film's end.*

Shirley Jones

APRIL LOVE, 1957 (ABOVE)

"The Waltons" meets Rebel Without a Cause *in this sentimental soaper about a troubled teen (Pat Boone) who is sent to serve probation on his uncle's farm in Kentucky after stealing a car. Most memorable for born-again-to-be Boone's shirtless rendition of the Oscar-nominated title song, the film packed just enough punch in its love scenes between Pat and sweet-singing Ivory-girl Jones to appeal to teenagers and their parents alike.*

Jayne Mansfield, 1957 (right)

Success may not have spoiled Rock Hunter, but it certainly did Monroe-clone Mansfield, here displaying a few of the considerable gifts that helped make her one of Tinseltown's hottest properties. Celebrating a pink Christmas alone in Hollywood, Mansfield would consolidate her sex-symbol image at the peak of her popularity the following year by marrying bodybuilder-turned-"B" actor Mickey Hargitay.

Ann Margret, 1960s (above)

*Promoted as a sort of sex-kitten counterpart to Elvis Presley,
the hard-working Swedish-born singer/dancer/actress had yet to
demonstrate any serious acting talent when this PR release-cum-Christmas
card was mailed out early in her career. Paired with the King in the 1964
camp classic* Viva Las Vegas, *the real-life Las Vegas headliner prefers
quiet times at home in the Hollywood Hills with her longtime
husband and personal manager, Roger Smith.*

Elvis Presley, 1957 (right)

*By the end of 1957, the pelvis-swinging singing sensation with
the rockabilly sound had already made three of the over thirty movies that,
as a whole, would represent the most commercially successful series of musicals
ever produced by Hollywood. Celebrating his last Christmas at home before
entering the army ("Elvis died when he went into the army," John Lennon
would one day quip), the King would be overshadowed after his return
to civilian life by the "British invasion" led by the Beatles.*

Anita Page, c. 1929

*The young MGM "featured player" born Anita Pomares in
Flushing, Queens, poses Mary Pickford-style for a typical studio
publicity release of the day. Featuring the chauvinistic tag line
"Look at the many nice things she got for being a good girl," Page
wasn't quite good enough and retired from the screen forever in 1936.*

Vera Miles and Murray Hamilton
THE FBI STORY, 1959

*A Warner Bros. tribute to the studio's popular G-man flicks
of the 1930s, the film traces the history of the FBI from Prohibition
to the Cold War through the career of one of its agents (James
Stewart). Filled with thrill-packed fun in its action sequences, the
Mervyn LeRoy-directed picture is marred only by some boring "B"-
grade diversions into the lead characters' personal lives, including
this overly cozy—and overly long—holiday scene.*

Mara Lane and Dick Powell

SUSAN SLEPT HERE, 1954

Despite the casting of "America's sweetheart" (Debbie Reynolds) in the title role and some sentimental seasonal cheer, this standard-issue 1950s bedroom farce is hardly family fare for the holidays. An innuendo-packed story of a married screenwriter (Powell) who falls in love with a delinquent teenager (Reynolds), the overly cute musical comedy is most noteworthy as the only movie in film history to be narrated by an Oscar statuette!

Loretta Young and Jeff Chandler
BECAUSE OF YOU, 1952 (ABOVE)

Most memorable for its miscasting of the forty-something, convent-educated Young in the role of an ex-convict, this slickly-made soaper capitalized on women's-magazine conventions to pack in moviegoers hooked on melodrama of the worst kind. The tawdry tale of a one-time mobster's moll who marries a straitlaced guy (Hollywood he-man-of-the-moment Chandler) who dumps her when he discovers she's a parolee, the film ends predictably many Christmases (and a few drug deals) later when our heroine-with-a-past gets him back.

George Burns and Gracie Allen, 1935 (right)

The harebrained half of the celebrated comedy team always kept some mistletoe hanging in her Beverly Hills home, no matter what the season. Once commenting, "My husband will never chase another woman; he's too fine, too decent—too <u>old</u>," Allen was one of the most devoted spouses in Tinseltown and made only two of over thirty films (not to mention numerous radio gigs and a television series) without her cigar-smoking sidekick, best friend, and husband.

Ellen Drew and Dick Powell

CHRISTMAS IN JULY, 1940 (ABOVE)

When adman Powell is tricked into believing his truly awful coffee campaign has won him $25,000, he celebrates with a mid-summer "Christmas" spending spree that makes the real holiday seem like kid's stuff. The second film from wunderkind director Preston Sturges, this particularly screwy screwball comedy may not be as memorable as some of Sturges's later works (The Palm Beach Story, Sullivan's Travels), *but you'll never forget the picture's infamous ad slogan: "If you can't sleep, it's not the coffee—it's the bunk!"*

Randolph Scott and Ann Harding

CHRISTMAS EVE, 1947 (RIGHT)

This saccharine-sweet holiday treat about an old woman (Harding) whose three sons save her from being swindled was eventually re-released as Sinner's Holiday *in order to pull in larger (and more jaded) crowds. Essentially three vignettes sealed with a Christmas Eve reunion, the B-list film is worth watching for its A-one lineup, including George Raft, George Brent, and Joan Blondell.*

Elizabeth Taylor and Margaret O'Brien

LITTLE WOMEN, 1949 (ABOVE)

*A glossy Christmas-card remake of the 1933 George Cukor-directed
Katharine Hepburn vehicle, this Technicolor adaptation of the beloved novel by
Louisa May Alcott still surpasses the two versions that followed (1978, 1981).
Featuring Taylor, O'Brien, June Allyson, and Janet Leigh as the four
independent March girls, the sugarplum-sweet saga of sisterly love in pre-
Civil War-era New England is a holiday treat any time of the year.*

Frank Morgan

SHOP AROUND THE CORNER, 1940 (RIGHT)

*Not to be confused with the formulaic musical remake featuring
Judy Garland* (In the Good Old Summertime), *this twinkling
Christmastime charmer starring James Stewart and Margaret Sullavan
as two pen pals who fall in love is a perfect example of director Ernst Lubitsch's
legendary light touch. Called by* The New Yorker *magazine "one of the
most beautifully acted and paced romantic comedies ever made," the film
is sure to soften even the most hard-bitten Scrooge.*

Janet Leigh and Robert Mitchum
HOLIDAY AFFAIR, 1949

*Long before her marriage to Tony Curtis and her starring
moment in Hollywood's most celebrated shower scene, Leigh
was a handpicked MGM peaches-and-cream princess-to-be.
Cast in a number of that studio's romantic melodramas in the
1940s, the former College of the Pacific music major made movies
like this standard-fare Christmas-season love story (about a
widow who is courted by two competing men) sweeter
than all the candy canes in Tinseltown.*

Greer Garson and Richard Nichols

BLOSSOMS IN THE DUST, 1941

Quaintly promoted as the first movie to bring to the screen
"the full beauty of Miss Garson's Irish coloring," this exquisitely filmed
early Technicolor production lost out to How Green Was My Valley
for Best Picture but won for Art Direction. Playing the real-life Edna
Gladney, a Texas woman who founded an orphanage after losing her
only child, the flame-haired Ulster-born beauty brought star power
(and a bit of color) to this otherwise shameless tearjerker from MGM.

Myrna Loy, Joan Holland, and William Powell

THE GREAT ZIEGFELD, 1936

The story of the rise of Broadway's most famous impresario
from a sideshow promoter to the toast of The Great White Way,
the project was eventually picked up by MGM, which lavished all of the
big-budget resources it could muster to produce a suitably gargantuan
entertainment. Nominated for six Academy Awards (winning three,
for Best Picture, Best Actress (Luise Rainer), and Best Dance Direction),
the three-hour extravaganza features future First Lady Pat Ryan
(Nixon) among a cast of thousands and magnificent sets that do
justice to the showman's legendary excess (including a
memorable carnival-like Christmas celebration).

Bing Crosby, Danny Kaye, and Marjorie Reynolds
WHITE CHRISTMAS, 1954 (ABOVE)
HOLIDAY INN, 1942 (RIGHT)
*The song that earned Irving Berlin an Academy Award
("White Christmas") became one of America's all-time favorite Yuletide
standards, thanks to these two carbon-copy Christmas musicals starring
Bing Crosby. Although* White Christmas *boasted a bigger-budget
production and the added musical attraction of Rosemary Clooney, the
earlier picture more quaintly captured the spirit of the season and
fared better at the box-office when it opened at Radio City
Music Hall during the war-weary winter of 1942.*

The Three Stooges, 1940s

*Appearing in the longest-running series of comedies in the
history of sound films, the Howard brothers (Moe and Jerome), along
with Larry Fine, ventured into feature films only after the release of their
two-reelers on TV garnered newfound popularity for the comedy team in
the late 1950s. Milking a few Yuletide yuks in this bit of song-and-dance
slapstick, the eye-gouging, nose-tweeking Brooklyn-born trio made
three of the unlikeliest Saint Nicks this side of the North Pole.*

Our Gang (The Little Rascals), 1936

*Hired by producer Hal Roach more for their physical
attributes than acting abilities, the "Our Gang" kids went through
several incarnations that helped to reinvigorate the long-running series.
Premiering in 1922 with Jackie Coogan, the pint-size costar of Charlie
Chaplin's* The Kid, *the comedy team peaked in the mid-1930s (their
short* Bored of Education *won an Oscar in 1936) with a cast led by
George "Spanky" McFarland, Darla Hood, Billie "Buckwheat" Thomas,
Eugene "Porky" Lee, and Carl "Alfalfa" Switzer. Here spreading a
little mischievous holiday cheer in one of their 221 one- and two-reel
shorts, the MGM-owned "Our Gang" became "The Little Rascals"
after Roach sold 100 of the shorts to television in 1955.*

Jeff Gillen and Peter Billingsley
A CHRISTMAS STORY, 1983 (ABOVE)
*Directed (incredibly) by the creator of the Porky's films, this
charming story of a much-put-upon kid (Billingsley) who wants nothing
more than a Red Ryder BB gun for Christmas is a modern-day holiday
classic. Featuring hilarious scenes of childhood trauma that any youngster
can relate to (including a harrowing encounter with a department-store
Santa), the picture will amuse adults as well—especially the sly narration
by Jean Shepherd, author of the novel upon which the film is based*
(In God We Trust, All Others Pay Cash).

Chevy Chase, Diane Ladd, and Beverly D'Angelo
NATIONAL LAMPOON'S CHRISTMAS VACATION, 1989 (RIGHT)
*He may be beaming with the Christmas spirit, but Chase is far
from funny in this Christmastime turkey from director John Hughes.
The third installment in the National Lampoon "Vacation" series,
the further misadventures of the Griswold family will amuse only
those who don't mind a bit of profanity and scatological humor
served up for the holiday season.*

Lucille Ball
YOURS, MINE AND OURS, 1968
When a widower with ten children marries a widow with eight in this hilarious harbinger of "The Brady Bunch," there's enough chaos and commotion to fill ten "I Love Lucy" episodes. A vehicle perfectly suited to the talents of its zany red-headed star (even if she is a bit old to get pregnant at 57!), the picture is based on the real-life adventures of a San Francisco couple who apparently didn't know when to stop.

47

Shirley Temple and James Dunn

BRIGHT EYES, 1934

One of curly Shirley's first starring pictures, this Twentieth Century-Fox crowd-pleaser was one of an amazing nine films churned out in 1934 by the dimple-cheeked charmer (she won an unprecedented special Oscar that year for her efforts). A syrupy-sweet saga of an orphan torn between foster parents, the movie features every Shirley-lover's favorite Temple tune: "On the Good Ship Lollipop."

Natalie Wood, Edmund Gwenn, and John Payne

MIRACLE ON 34TH STREET, 1947

Is he or isn't he? That's the question that is finally brought to trial in this enduring classic about a Macy's department-store Santa who claims he is the real Kris Kringle. Among the disbelievers is the eight-year-old former Natasha Gurdin, who, in her fourth film, gives one of her most memorable performances in a career that spanned almost forty years. It was long-time British stage actor Gwenn, however, who became an overnight sensation and picked up an Oscar for his middle-aged star turn as Tinseltown's most memorable Saint Nick.

Reginald Owen
A CHRISTMAS CAROL, 1938

One of the half-dozen film adaptations of the beloved Charles Dickens tale about a miser who is reformed after he is visited by four ghosts on Christmas Eve, this early MGM production gets top prizes for its superb acting and well-mounted sets. Starring the long-time British character actor as the infamous Christmas curmudgeon, the picture also features some particularly spooky spirits who help scare the dickens out of Scrooge.

Alastair Sim, above and far right, and Michael Hordern
A CHRISTMAS CAROL, 1951
The most critically acclaimed film version of Dickens's holiday classic
is also the most faithful adaptation of the novel. Titled Scrooge *in*
Great Britain, *where it originally premiered, the superbly acted effort*
stars the Scottish-born one-time stage player, actor, producer, and
director in a tour-de-force performance as the most human—and
moving—Ebenezer Scrooge ever committed to celluloid.

Albert Finney, above and near left, and Kenneth More

SCROOGE, 1970

If you like your Dickens set to music, this version of his yuletide classic might be just the ticket. Originally starring Richard Harris and then Rex Harrison (who both dropped out), the film was Scrooge-less until Finney joined up less than three weeks before shooting began. Although the infamous English miser's money-grubbing ways put to music may not be everyone's cup of tea, the picture did big box-office business on both sides of the Atlantic and picked up Oscar nominations for Best Song ("Thank You Very Much"), Art Direction, Score, and Costumes.

Reginald Owen and Terry Kilburn

A CHRISTMAS CAROL, 1938

*One of the most popular child stars of the 1930s, the
eleven-year-old British-born Kilburn made an auspicious film
debut in this lavish MGM version of the Dickens favorite. His performance as a memorably sweet-natured Tiny Tim charmed American
audiences—not to mention Owen's snarling Scrooge—by the end
of this enchanting holiday-season heart-warmer.*

**Gene Lockhart, Kathleen Lockhart, June Lockhart,
Terry Kilburn, Lynne Carver, and players**
A CHRISTMAS CAROL, 1938
*The acting Lockhart clan turned out en masse for this sentimental
family favorite from Metro-Goldwyn-Mayer. Featuring the movie
debut of twelve-year-old future TV mom June Lockhart ("Lassie,"
"Lost in Space"), this second film adaptation of the Charles Dickens story
was one of over a hundred silent and sound screen appearances by Gene
Lockhart, the Canadian-born former vaudevillian, veteran stage
performer, writer, and patriarch of the Hollywood acting dynasty.*

Bill Murray and Carol Kane

SCROOGED, 1988

*With cameo appearances by everyone from Buddy Hackett and
Bobcat Goldthwait to Robert Goulet and Mary Lou Retton, it's more
fun to play Spot the Stars than take this rowdy remake of the Victorian
classic seriously. As the Ghost of Christmas Present, Kane is outrageous
confronting modern-day Scrooge Murray (this time a venal TV exec) in
one of the few inspired comedic turns in this story that ends incongruously
with an impassioned holiday-season sermon by the film's star.*

Ray Bolger, Annette Funicello, and Tommy Sands

BABES IN TOYLAND, 1961

*Despite a great cast and Disney's best special effects, this
less-than-magical remake of the 1934 Laurel and Hardy version
of the beloved Victor Herbert operetta is no match for the original. The
story of a holiday-hating heavy, Barnaby Barnacle (a miscast Bolger),
who tries to destroy the mythical town of Toyland, the children's classic
was updated once more in 1986 (with Drew Barrymore and
Keanu Reeves) with even more disappointing results.*

**Charlotte Henry, Felix Knight, Oliver Hardy,
Stan Laurel, and Henry Brandon**
BABES IN TOYLAND, 1934

*As Stanley Dum and Oliver Dee (a pair of mismatched wooden soldiers),
Tinseltown's most celebrated comedy duo rescues Bo Peep (Henry) and
Tom Tom (Knight) from the clutches of Barnaby of Bogeyland (Brandon)
and saves Toyland forever. An eccentric minor classic from producer Hal
Roach, this original film version of the Victor Herbert operetta boasts a
classic Christmastime finale ("March of the Wooden Soldiers") and
inspired two sequels that were twice as long but only half as much fun.*

Bob Hope and William Frawley, center

THE LEMON DROP KID, 1951

The number-one box-office star of 1949, Hope was still riding the wave of his enormous film popularity when he played the title character in this remake of the Damon Runyon story first filmed in 1934 with Lee Tracy in the lead. The madcap tale of an incompetent racetrack bookie (Hope) who owes money to the mob, the picture features a side-splitting Santa Claus sequence and a stable of some of Hollywood's most talented character actors (including Frawley, who had costarred in the Paramount original).

Dudley Moore

SANTA CLAUS, 1985

Referred to everywhere as Santa Claus: The Movie *(except
in the title credits on-screen!), this venal version of the Santa Claus
legend was recommended by* Variety *magazine "for children of all ages,
but particularly the infantile or senile." Costarring Burgess Meredith
and John Lithgow (as an evil New York City toy manufacturer), the
cartoon-like fantasy will delight fans of the mischievous Moore,
an appropriately puny prodigal elf who forsakes the North Pole
for the demon ways of the Big Apple.*

**John Call, Leonard Hicks, Vincent Beck,
Donna Conforti, and Pia Zadora**

SANTA CLAUS CONQUERS THE MARTIANS, 1964

Appropriately listed in the book The Fifty Worst Movies of
All Time, *this staple of the midnight cult-movie circuit is a camp
classic that is truly out of this orbit. The pseudo-sci-fi story of a group of
Martians who abduct Santa Claus because they don't have one of their
own, this low-budget experiment in celluloid lunacy features that
real-life space cadet and sometime sexpot starlet Pia Zadora in her
seminal screen role (as an alien child from outer space).*

Dennis Morgan, Barbara Stanwyck, and Reginald Gardiner

CHRISTMAS IN CONNECTICUT, 1945

Playing a Martha Stewart-like character in this holiday-season staple costarring Morgan and Gardiner as two competing husbands-to-be, Stanwyck reveals her flair for comedy as a phony advice columnist who must conjure up a scene of domestic perfection in the name of publicity. The fact that the star isn't married, can't cook, and doesn't own the charming country house she says she does provides a steady stream of side-splitting laughs from beginning to end. The film was remade for cable TV in 1992 (Arnold Schwarzenegger's directorial debut!) with Dyan Cannon in the lead.

The Reagans, 1959

*The one-time radio announcer, "B" actor, and host of
television's General Electric Theatre poses for a little Tinseltown PR
at home with his family in Pacific Palisades, California. A Christmas-
card-perfect image of 1950s domestic tranquility, the future Governor
of California and his family were among the most
esteemed residents of America's movie capital.*

Frances Rafferty, 1943

'Tis the season to be sexy for this MGM starlet-in-training.
From the studio that put the tinsel in Tinseltown, this standard-fare
publicity pic, shot by MGM's premier lensman, Clarence Sinclair Bull,
featured a tag line guaranteed to arouse a little holiday spirit:
"Mail a letter to Santa Claus, and he might just send the
Irish beauty to grace your home for Christmas!"

CREDITS AND SOURCES

PROJECT EDITOR: J. C. SUARÈS
TEXT: J. SPENCER BECK
PICTURE EDITOR: LESLIE FRATKIN